Dedication

I would like to dedicate this book to my sister Teresa Jones, whom is battling ALS. She is a winner despite the obstacles.

I want to thank my mother Frances Donald better known as my backbone. She is always encouraging me not to give up along with my other siblings.

I want reserve a special thanks to Angela Powell for being that spot of sunshine during a period in my life when I was really in pain.

I want to express a special dedication to all women that are going through life feeling like there is no way out and when life seems to weigh you down, just keep pushing.

 Remember, that if you can take the pull, God will pull you out.

 Last but not least, my coworker, good friend, motivator, and the editor of this book, Olivia Crump. She encouraged and motivated me to write and tell my testimony.

Above all, I thank God for bringing me through all my struggles and teaching me that I can stand on my own two feet with His help.

April Showers

Memories of a Survivor

Written by April Donald

To protect the identity of others, names have been changed.

Chapter One

Loaded Dice

Who we choose to love may not always be the one that chooses to love us. Thinking back, I really thought I knew what was real. I didn't know what love was and I surely didn't know how to find it. I was young and clueless but when an opportunity came knocking on my door, I answered...

He was a handsome, well put together guy. Robert worked every day with his father on a house next door. I watched him wishing to meet him. But I thought to myself, "I'm too afraid to say something to him, besides he has a girlfriend."Finally I got the courage to go out and at least be noticed. I was so surprised! It worked. He yelled out to me but I was so shy I didn't respond. I didn't really know how to show him what I was feeling and had been feeling since the first day I saw him. But as time went on, we began to get acquainted. His girlfriend and I attended college together. I wanted to bump her completely out of the way. I really didn't know what I was asking for but I had a plan. I dropped one of my classes so I could synchronize my schedule to spend more time with Robert. We met privately every chance we could get. I fell in love and I believed he loved me. It didn't take long for him to decide he wanted to commit to me only. I didn't know then that if a man creeps with you, he will probably creep on you. He would allow me to ride in his girlfriend's car. Robert did her wrong but I was so glad to get him, I didn't care. I thought he was a prize. Little did I realize, he didn't respect women.

As I reflect on it, I can see the damage this caused her and me. She was so upset when he told her about me; she cut him across the face. At the time, I'm thinking "crazy bitch". I know now she must have loved him too. But I wanted him and at that time, that's all that mattered.

We started making plans to have a life together. We struggled but I was so very much in love with this man. I helped him get a job at my place of employment. I was proud to have this man. I idolized him. I enjoyed working with him even though he was a bit controlling at times. We rode the bus to work together and we were so in love.

One big thing that did get on my nerves as I remember, Robert kept asking everyone how much money they made for the day. We worked at a casino and tips were very good. I wished he would've stop doing that and acting like he wasn't used to anything. But I kept forgetting, he wasn't use to anything. This was his first real job.

We decided to move in together. We moved in a boarding house. It wasn't much of a place. We had to share the bathroom with others but as long as we were together, we didn't mind this at all.

One day Robert asked me to prove my love for him. He wanted me to have his baby. He didn't have children and wanted a child of his own. I already had one child that was in the care of my mother. Why did I say yes? I ignored all the signs screaming No! We planned this romantic candlelit moment to toss away all my birth control pills. This marked the day of conception. Two months later, I found out I was pregnant. We decided we needed to find a house. We were anticipating on starting our new family.

I was very ill during my pregnancy, so I quit my job and stayed at home. Robert took on the responsibility of paying our living expenses. Then our landlord decided he wanted the house back. We had to move out. I had to move back in with my mother and he moved back in with his mother also. We were apart for the first time since we met. I was so miserable living back home. There were times I barely had money for food and gas. Many nights I just went to bed hungry. Things did get better eventually. We managed to find an apartment but had to wait awhile to move in because it needed repairs. This was the longest wait ever. Every day I was asking about it wanting to know if it was ready. Finally, Robert came to my mom's house with the big news. We were so broke but I was excited to get my own place. We moved with very little but we were happy.

I was sick a lot. During this time, my mom wanted me to get my oldest son and move him in with me. This was a really bad time. I wasn't ready for that responsibility. Robert and I didn't have the basic necessities to live. To top it off, we were practically eating noodles every day. But I still prepared to have my baby. I accumulated things I needed from other people. Things slowly came together.

Robert was showing me he loved me but it was something just a bit strange to me. You know that thing you can't quite seem to put your finger on. He continued to look and dress nice. But I barely had clothes. Come to think of it, sure would have been nice to go to the beauty salon every once in a while instead of a kitchen hair do. But I sacrificed. I gave so much of me until I had nothing left of myself. I couldn't see what this relationship was doing to my self-esteem and self-worth.

After I gave birth, things began to change. He began to hang out giving phony alibis to his whereabouts. He always had the excuse that he was running late coming home. We formed this love hate relationship. We would break up just to make up. I was putting him out and then accepting him back. This was exhausting. The very last argument we had, Robert didn't repeat the cycle we had been going through. I didn't hear from him.

So I called his job wondering what was going on to keep him away. As crazy as it may sound, I actually wanted this fool to come back. He was all I knew and I still wanted him…Robert continued talking telling me he was seeing someone else. He referred to her as being a grown woman as if to say I'm a little girl or something. I couldn't believe what was happening. I knew all along something wasn't right but I didn't want to believe it. I was so hurt. I cried while he was still talking. He told me she drove a nice car and had a nice house. I felt so small to hear this man that I sacrificed everything for tell me what some other woman had. Then if that wasn't enough, he tells me to stop crying, straighten up and take it like a real woman. How heartless and cruel could he be? But then this is the kind of man I have always had in him, I just couldn't see it because at the time I was the chosen one.

I cried for days. My heart was crushed. I didn't have the strength to even be a mom to my children. I would put them to bed early every night. I had no energy. I couldn't even walk through my house. I would crawl dragging my very soul across the floor. I would have the house completely quiet laying on the sofa just in case he decided to come back. I wanted to make sure I would hear his knock on the door.

Finally I went to the doctor for a checkup because I was just losing too much weight but nothing was physically wrong. I was sick from a broken heart. The only cure for that was time and prayer. Each day I would think of him being with someone else and I would cry all over again. All our dreams of getting married, buying a home, a nice family car and being a real family was all a lie. It was hard to move on because this relationship that he had with this other woman was the talk of the town. I heard he was going all out for her and really building a life with her. This pushed me further into depression. I laid awake at night thinking about the day we decided to have a baby. How could he just leave us like that? I didn't understand why my life ended up like this. I began to pray and ask God to deliver me from all the pain.

One night I felt like getting out. I began to feel a little strength so I went to a football game with a friend. We got out of the car and I looked up and saw him with that woman. Suddenly those feelings came over me and without thought, I yelled out his name. He was so mean. He yelled back and asked me, "What the Fuck do you want," as if I never meant anything to him ever. I broke down right there on the spot.

I got back in the car and just passed out in the floor of the car with hurt. My friend was trying so hard to help me. She was calling my name and I just couldn't express to her how bad I felt. I got up and got another view of them but this time they were riding by in her truck and he was driving.

Soon after my mom called wanting me to pick up my children. It was time to try to be a mom with no energy again. I drove to my mom's house to pick up my babies in tears. When I got there I wanted so badly for her to reach out to me but instead she just said, "You will be okay. Get you something to drink." I just went on with a lump in my throat. I knew I had to find a way to pick up and move on, because my children needed me.

I somehow had to find a way to get over my love for this man but still allow him to see our child. How was I going to continue to deal with him? I found my way with God's help. He was just so lowdown. He bought really nice things for our son but wouldn't allow him to bring them home. He could enjoy them at his house only. I was doing the best I could as a single mom but couldn't give my son what he was getting at his dad's house. But then I realized I gave him love. I picked myself up, took care of my children and began to move on with my life. I started getting out with my friends and gradually I liked myself again. I began to take care of me.

One day I got a visit from my neighbor. She brought me the newspaper to read. It was news about Robert and his arrest. I was in a state of shock. He had been charged with armed robbery, stealing electronics for his new girlfriend. I immediately called his mom and she gave me details.

I wanted to see him. I don't know why really. I think a part of me wanted to see him in a vulnerable state and I also wanted him to see how well I was doing without him. I dressed my best and paid him a visit. Waiting for him to come, all kinds of thoughts were going through my head.

He came in where I was waiting. I looked at him from head to toe. This man that dressed to impress was now wearing an orange jumpsuit. He sat down behind the glass and picked up the phone. He began to cry. He told me how sorry he was and I just had to interrupt him. I said, "Straighten up and take it like a man!" My blood had begun to boil as I had a flash back of how mean he was to me. I walked out and left him sitting there crying. I visited a few more times and I believe I did because he is my child's father. I didn't have the desire to turn my back on him like he deserved. But after a while, I stopped visiting. It was truly time to put the past behind me. He is currently serving a twenty year sentence.

All while I was going through with this man believing he was my world, believing I could not go another day without him, I didn't realize I was blessed that he left me. You see, some may not think life is a gamble. Well it is but God gave me loaded dice and I was playing a fixed game. In the end I am a winner. I was always winning every time Robert walked away. God protected me from a life that would not have been good for my children and me. I appreciate that now and I'm so glad God knew best.

Chapter two

Player's Club

Nothing can get you back on track and focused better than a girl's night out. I was headed home after painting the town red when this guy approached me. He introduced himself as Lester. I admit I was grinning quite hard. Before I knew it, I had given him my address. "Imma get at you later." he said. Even though I had been through my share of disappointments, I must admit the thought of male companionship was missing from my life. I wanted to try again. Maybe this time I will meet Mr. Right.

Well, are you curious to know if I did? Follow along with me as I continue my story...

The next day a white Monte Carlo came through the apartment complex with rims and a glistening paint job gaining my undivided attention. I knew immediately it was a gentleman caller. I really didn't expect him to show up so soon. But I was blushingly excited to see him. I walked over to the car and we exchanged pleasantries leading to him inquiring about my schedule. He was interested in a date. Luckily I was off that day which was perfect timing. We made plans to see each other later that day. I dashed off to prepare hurriedly finishing all my daily chores. I wanted to make sure my evening was clear for my new acquaintance. Finally I'm relaxing and just waiting when I noticed the weather was not looking so good. It looked as if it would rain. I started to feel some disappointment because to me that meant plans may have to be put on hold. And there it was….. rain pouring.

I decided to go ahead and start dinner for the children still hoping the rain would stop. The phone rang. Much to my surprise it was Lester. He called to confirm our date. He mentioned the weather and how hard it was raining. But still he had intentions to come over. I really wanted to see him. Not sure why, but I do know I wanted someone to hold at this point in my life.

I put the children to bed. As it was getting past the time we agreed, I began to feel he may not show, especially since the weather was getting worse. Suddenly there was a knock on the door. I opened it and there stood Lester dripping wet. He walked to my place because of car trouble. He didn't let that stop him from coming. Wow! I felt so special. I invited him in. It was an evening of cuddling and getting to know each other. We decided to see each other again. We were inseparable. Every day we saw each other. Lester shared with me his dream to become a rapper. He had a desire to move us all to California. He proved his love for us with the time he spent with my children and me. We went shopping, on carriage rides, just a fairy tale love affair. I believed he was the one.

One day there was a strange knock on the door. It was two ladies asking for Lester. I didn't tell them he was there because of the feeling I had about them. Also I looked out and there was the white Monte Carlo, the car that was supposedly out of commission.

After dismissing them, I went back inside to confront Lester. I needed just a few questions answered. In my heart I wanted so desperately for him to clear up my doubts. But my intuition spelled out "CHEATER". Before I could get the questions out, he immediately told me one of the women was his ex-girlfriend.

He went on to tell me that she shared ownership of the car with him. He wanted to sell it but she didn't. His story sounded convincing. We sealed the discussion with passionate lovemaking. Afterwards, he rubbed my hair as if it was a prelude to something he wanted to say….

"I may have to leave," were the words that fell from his lips. I couldn't believe what he was saying. He explained he wouldn't get the contract he desired. So he needed to go look up a friend to reside until he could get on his feet and pursue his dream. He continued with desperate sobs of his ex-girlfriend blocking the sale of the car making it impossible for him to stay. I didn't want him to go. I found love again and I didn't want to lose it. Clearing my throat, I asked him how much money he needed. He responded saying, "twenty-five hundred." He assured me he could turn this amount into a profit in no time. After a moment of silence, he asked me if he could borrow it from me. I had anticipated a pretty decent tax refund that year and I was holding it for things my children and I needed. I was so vulnerable at this moment but I felt good about this man so I agreed. I also had plans to buy a car but I placed that on hold to help him.

I kept this decision to myself. I didn't want my family and friends to know. When I received my check, I loaned him the money as promised. My children needed things and I had expenses I needed to catch up so badly. I was riding to work with others but I gave him this money as an act of love believing he would make good on it. After receiving the money, it didn't end there He needed more from me. He wanted to rent a car to go to Memphis. Believe it or not! I gave him more money all in the name of love. We headed to Memphis. I funded the trip because I really believed in him. He performed his business and we headed back to Mississippi. I held on to the promise that he was going to pay back the money and buy me a car.

My bills were due and I reluctantly asked him for help and each time he did what he could without hesitation. My brother quickly reminded me he was just giving me back my own money. Eventually he did make good on the money and made a profit. We went car shopping as he promised. Although I liked the car he bought for me, it wasn't as nice as the car he bought for himself. Still I was okay. I reassured myself that as long as I was a part of his life, all was well.

Lester moved in with me. There were good and bad days. Due to more car problems, I had to ride the transit to and from work. I worked the three to eleven shift and because of the many stops, I would make it home about one in the morning.

Now I am thinking all I want at this hour is to go to a quiet home and rest. Instead there are about five to six guys gambling, throwing dice, and talking loud. Grown men were on my sofa playing video games. I stormed passed them to my bedroom going through clouds of weed smoke. I didn't like any of this but Lester treated me well so I dealt with it.

He loved to buy things for me. We went shopping and out to clubs all the time. We went on road trips and had amazing times together.

I quickly learned, things not meant for you giving you a false sense of security will come to an end.

Lester was quite the ladies man. He began to hang out often with so call friends. My suspicions started to arise. One day I had a visitor. It was a woman named Alicia. She really came at an awkward time. I was washing my hair and doing things around the house. It was a laid back day and I was home alone relaxing.

However I invited her in because she peaked my curiosity. She was looking for Lester to buy weed from him. Of course I told her he wasn't there and she left quietly. In the back of my mind, I felt there was more to that visit so I did a little investigating, if nothing more but to just lay my suspicions to rest. My mom had a saying she use to say, "Set the rope, stand back and watch the dog hang himself."

This same woman and her friends followed me when I drove his car. They had the nerve to spray paint his car. This situation had grown out of control. At the club, if she was there, Lester would be distant from me. I had a strange desire to fight for him. I didn't know what I was taking on. I believed he loved me and I believed that he was worth fighting for.

This woman would leave messages on my answering machine disrespecting me. I would turn to him and all he would say is it's just someone playing on the phone denying it was that woman. But I knew it was her. I was growing weary of this back and forth drama.

I was so tired of not knowing. I wanted the truth. Was this just a woman after my man or was Lester involved with this woman? Oh God! I would pray. "Show me what I need to know. Give me a peace of mind."

One rainy Saturday, I will never forget, He announced he was going out with friends, which meant I would be home alone on a weekend night. He put on his best suit of clothes, cologne, gave me a hug and a kiss and left. For some reason, I could not rest that night. I was up pacing the floor.

I had a gut intuition and I had to find out where it would lead me. I called my friend to give me a ride to Jonestown. She agreed and was on the way. I had the address to that same woman. She lived near an alley. We pulled up and low and behold, what do we see? His car was parked in the alley of this trollop. I asked God immediately for strength because I was so mad and hurt. I jumped out of my friend's car and since I had keys to his car I decided to take it in a rage to get even. I set the alarm off and he looked out the window and saw me take the car.

Later I got pulled over because the car was reported stolen. I put on my charm and told the police it was my boyfriend's car. I explained I was picking it up. They chalked it off to some kind of misunderstanding and allowed me to go on. Lester did not come home for two days.

Upon returning home, he lied to me with a story that he was conducting business with his brother. You would think that just because he was gone for days would be enough for me. But I reached a little deeper in my heart, dismissed what I saw and forgave him.

Don't ask God to show you what you already know especially if you are not going to do anything about the situation. I know that now.

I found out later this woman had the same coat and outfits he bought me. I was just drowning in more truth. There were more calls from more women. I found out he was dating a woman right there in the neighborhood. People were telling me that they were involved. Tennis shoes night was a trend in Clarksdale at the night club. Lester loved to go to this with his new shoes because he was quite the show off. Word got to me to lay low and watch things closely on this night.

So the night arrived and Lester made plans to go with his friends which didn't bother me because I had plans to roll out with my friends too. I knew in the pit of my stomach I would see more to hurt me but I went on anyway. I was at the club drinking and partying with my girls and Lester did show up with his friends.

I was happy at first because so far so good. But then it happened…..My neighbor Sasha walked in and I couldn't notice anything but her shoes. She had on an identical pair to Lester's. I was in love true enough but I was not stupid to believe this was just a coincidence. I wanted to cry but I held back the "April Showers" and went on the dance floor to dance with him. I quickly noticed he was staring at her but he was in such a zone, he didn't notice me watching him, while he was staring at her with lust in his eyes. I didn't say a word because it took all my energy to hold back tears.

The next day Lester picks an argument with me. He kept on saying he was going to get his own place on several occasions. This time when he said it, in an instant of anger, I told him to go ahead and do it. This was going just as he had planned. This man had lied to me, cheated on me and I forgave him and stayed with him. Now he's the one leaving me. This man moved next door with Sasha. It was not only hurtful, but humiliating. My children would see him and ask constant questions grasping for their own answers to what happened. He would be outside playing with her children and would ignore mine as if he never knew them. I was in so much pain from this experience. I turned to drinking to try and ease the pain but it didn't help me. I would see them leaving the house doing all the things he did with me.

Every dog has its day….. Sasha was a casino employee and she had stolen a large sum of money. It began to become clear to me. Lester was an opportunist. I began to reflect back on when we first met and I remember being in that same position. I had something to offer him. Lester is only in for a ride. He will be with her until the next door of opportunity presents itself and all the while he is with her he will be fishing. I remember another saying my mom use to say, "There's no need to talk to anyone about your man problems because when you get tired, you will walk away."

I didn't know how to keep up the lifestyle I had grown accustom. I allowed my thoughts to take me to doing something I knew was wrong. His customers would still come by for business. Now you use your own imagination to what you think they were looking for but after a few times, I decided I would make me some money, I had a little clientele and this helped me to keep things I liked to do going. But it started to get too much for me and I came to my senses to realize I am a mother. I don't want this lifestyle to cause me to lose my children. I woke up and ended this and made up in my mind I was going to make it without that fast life and fast way of making money. I decided to go to school to become a Certified Nurse's Assistant. I got a job and worked in the field for about two years and was doing well. I was strong and had gotten over Lester.

During this time I encouraged my friend to go to Dealer School. I went also and put in an application. It was also the day for drug screening. I was given my cup to give the urine and I proceeded to give the specimen. The lady in charge threw it in the garbage and said it wasn't enough. She instructed me to give more. I had been smoking a little weed and was nervous to give more. I sat there and told her I couldn't go anymore. Finally I told her I needed to go pick up my children. I left there knowing I blew my chances of more money and benefits for my family. My stomach was sick and I began to cry. Although I had a job, it wasn't nearly the money I needed to do the nice things I use to do. I had an eye for high rollers. I could catch one too. This was always the way I knew to have that money rolling in. So this was a chance for me to get it on my own and I blew it. Every day I would get off work, pick up my children, stop by the liquor store and go home depressed. I continued this routine for several days not knowing when it would be a better day.

One rainy day I was picking up my children as I always did. I stopped at the store to get food and then headed home. I was having such a hard time getting the babies out of the car in the rain.

They were age two and four. It was so hard being a single parent. I made it inside the house, dried off the children and myself. I put a frozen pizza in the oven and began to unwind to listen to my messages. I got some old off the wall message proceeded by some other nothing special to listen to messages. I was about to press the button to just stop listening but I went on to hear them all. The last message was from the casino. It was informing me that I was accepted to Dealer School. I fell to the floor in tears but this time, April's Shower had brought in some flowers. This was truly a miracle that I had been chosen in spite of that drug screening day. I was so happy, thanking God the rest of the night.

Chapter three

Midnight Hour

The darkest hour before day…..

The first order of business was figuring out how I was going to get to dealer school, pick up my children from school and get to my present job too.

There were three ladies in my class from Clarksdale that graciously offered to give me a ride to school. After school they would drop me off at my job, where I would wait in the break room for three hours until my shift started. My mom had agreed to pick up my children and keep them until I got off work. I would get off work at eleven and ride the transit to my car, which was not in well enough shape to do the whole trip. I would then take my car to my mom's and pick up my children and back home about two in the morning. This was my exhausting routine for six weeks.

There were all kinds of struggles the fifth week...

My mom decides she can't pick up the children any more stressing me to no end. I can remember just accepting what she said and just storming out of her house. Later she decides to continue to help.

Why did that happen?

Then in that same week, my teacher pulls me to the side to tell me I am falling behind and must do better or she will have to drop me from the class. I pulled myself together to study even harder. I was so tired but I did it.

The day came when I had to audition to be a dealer. I got up that morning in my black and white attire. I headed off to school with promise in my spirit, hope in my heart and a prayer in my soul. They began to call us in groups alphabetically. I was in the first group. I went in and did what I knew was my best at that audition.

Later the teacher comes in to announce who made it. I was so nervous. She comes in holding both her hands together as she perched her lips and said to us…

"Welcome Aboard"

"I made it. I'm a dealer," I said over and over. I was so happy. Good income for my children and me. I would be making a considerable amount more than I was. I still had to go to my other job. I couldn't wait for that shift to be over.

I was resting in the break room with my head resting on the table. I was awaken by a man's voice. He asked me did my man have my car dropping me off early every day. I raised my head with pride to tell him I have been in school and today I became a dealer. He congratulated me and I went back to my nap. I felt so good saying that. This was an accomplishment for me. I was able to say I did this without the help of some man.

I did this for my children and me. With God's help I did this.

After my shift, I couldn't get to my mother's house fast enough to give her the good news. I made it there and announced my success.

"I will be picking up my badge and start working as a dealer," I happily said.

I received really nice money and I could finally see myself to making it getting nice things for my children. Most of all, I would make it on my own. I decided it was time for a change for my children and me.

Chapter four

The Wrong Side of Love

Still Smiling in the Midst of my Storm, my sister moved from Nashville to Clarksdale with me. We both decided to move to Memphis. We made an agreement to help each other and not abandon each other until things were good for us both. It was exciting and we both had great expectations for the future. Starting my new job at the casino and now living in a new area, I really didn't know many people. Later, I met a really nice guy, Grant…

We started talking about my move. He offered to show me around. We began to ride to work together which I enjoyed.

Hesitantly, I started going out with this guy. He seemed harmless. My history with men had not been the best but we were just friends. My family loved him. He had a great sense of humor. My children loved hanging out with him. We grew very close. He went to great lengths to make me happy, but the down to this was he was married. He and his wife were having marital issues. When he met me, he felt appreciated and loved. Before we realize what was happening, we fell in love.

I've never believed in dating a married man. In fact I was against it. This started out as a friendship and love slipped in. His wife moved out and eventually my children and I moved from my sister in with him. I was happy with him but it was still in my mind that he was married. However he treated me like a queen.

And before you pass judgment, don't do so without imagining living a moment of what I been through. Maybe there are some ladies that know exactly what I'm talking about. I had been through hell and I felt I deserved some happiness by any means necessary. He respected me and this was something I never had from a man. I had a great job, a great guy and life was starting to look up.

But here's the twist...

I went out a lot and I enjoyed life with zeal but I was doing all this without Grant. I just kind of forgot he was in my life. I got caught up in the moment. Although he was giving me the world, I felt I was missing out on something. I also believe that because I knew he was married, I was afraid to commit. I was consumed with the idea that he may accept his wife back. Thinking of what I had already been through, I just couldn't be hurt again. I was confused and didn't know what to do. I would be gone so much; Grant would come to the club looking for me. He would plead for me to come home. I was drowning in having fun while he would be home with my boys. I would shop for a new outfit and head for the club. It really wasn't anything in that club for me. I don't know what I was trying to escape. Grant would buy me roses and "just because" gifts trying his best to do what he could to bring me joy. He lived for an opportunity to tell someone how much he loved me. I remember one day before Grant went to work, he asked me to write down things I would like to have and give it to him when he returned. All I could think to write was things I wished for my children and me when I was struggling so badly. I wrote down a double wide refrigerator with name brand food in it. Also I wanted a washer and dryer. And lastly, I want a house that smelled like the fresh scent of Tide. I stopped writing and began to drift in thought to come back and write that I wanted to be loved and happy every day. I left the note on the computer so he could see it. The next day when I came home, he met me at the door to ask me to run an errand. When I returned, I smelled Tide. I walked in and saw a double wide refrigerator with of course all brand name foods inside. He also bought me a washer and dryer. He showed us love as much as he could every day.

 I had my friends in my ear that I needed to be careful and have a backup plan. Listening to my friends I began to mess-up what I had with Grant. I was so afraid that this man was going to hurt me like all the others, I could not enjoy him. I started to see someone else behind his back. I ruined what I had with Grant with this fling. I could not recognize what I had with Grant because of my past disappointments. The relationship ended and I moved out. Grant was so hurt. Shortly after, I left the casino where we worked together and found a job at another one. I decided to take a break from dating. I concentrated on getting my life together and focus more on my children. When I started my other dealer job, it was a little different. The clientele was older people and the atmosphere was a little slower. It was a laid back job and I enjoyed it. As time went on, dating was the farthest thing on my mind.

Even though it didn't work with Grant, I can say finally I met a man that treated me like I deserved to be treated. Sadly I couldn't embrace it. But you know what; I can say that was the best man I have ever had in my life.

Chapter five

The Invitation

As luck would have it, my job wasn't as exciting as I expected it to be, but I made the best of it. I met a lady that I bonded with and we started hanging out together.

This was fun because it took my mind off my past. It was something different. This young woman became like a sister to me. I embraced those times because it was a moment in my life of a cleansing from past pain and hurt. Six months into working my new job. I was taking a break from work when I noticed a guy staring at me. I really didn't make much of it but the looks continued. I was in deep thought one day when someone startled me. It was my coworker John. He was anxious to inform me of a guy that has been noticing me and had a desire to get to know me. I had no interest in getting to know anyone but John was quite persistent. I hesitantly agreed to exchange phone numbers with this admirer. I accepted an invitation to an after work gathering.

A few coworkers were meeting up for drinks and a little card playing. Sounded like fun to me, so I anticipated on going for a change of pace. Upon arrival, my admirer Chris walked in. Immediately we connected. He was courteous and attentive in making me feel comfortable.

I was impressed with his hospitality. From then on he greeted me every morning with a sweet text. I was still a little apprehensive about this whole scene because I had been down this road a few times only to be disappointed.

The next day I got a special message from a fellow coworker to sign up to leave early for the day. Chris had planned another gathering. This seemed crazy to me because I just started this job but the messenger quickly informed me that Chris was a supervisor which meant he could make it happen.

Indeed he did. I was leaving early and before I realized it, I was really happy to see him again. When I arrived at this place, he welcomed me introducing all his friends, again making me feel very welcome. I tried to really pay attention to this guy without being so obvious. He was really handsome, slightly arrogant but surprisingly that was a turn on. I began to mellow out and mingle. As it grew late, I excused myself from the evening thanking everyone for a great time. Before I could leave, Chris invited me on a road trip to Louisiana. In my mind, I'm thinking this guy really likes to do things. So I accepted his invitation again. My sister agreed to babysit and I prepared for the getaway. We loaded up, picked up his friends and headed for the highway. Talking a mile a minute, we were there before we knew it. We stopped for drinks and then to our hotel rooms.

The next day I was introduced to his best friend's family. They were having a cook out. I couldn't believe the fun we were having. I needed this time with a man. I had gone through so much. Some good clean fun was what the doctor ordered. At the end of the day, I was wondering how things would be with Chris once we returned home. I hoped in my heart this would last.

Back at work again, Chris was still the perfect gentlemen. He extended yet another invitation to his house after work, but this time he gave me a key thinking he would get off later and didn't want me to have to wait. I can't stress enough how much of a gentlemen this guy really was. I went on to his place finding it a little messy. So I decided to tidy up a bit. I even took it a step further and went to the store for a few items. In my heart, I really liked this guy and I guess I wanted it to be more without officially admitting it to myself.

Shortly after, Chris arrived home and thought he was in the wrong place. He greeted me with a hug and kiss thanking me several times. We spent the rest of the evening cuddling on into the next morning. He placed the key to his house in my hand. We continued to see each other. We did everything together. My family loved him. He bonded with my boys and finally I felt safe. As we grew closer, Chris moved in with us. Later my brother moved in also. We were a family. Chris made every effort to show me he wanted our relationship to work. I decided to give love another try.

Now, I know what you are thinking, but hold on because this is not the end...

Chapter six

Dr. Jekyll, Mr. Hyde

At what point is abuse really abuse? Why is that a question we as women ask when we already know the answer.

Why is this something we often deny?

Well if you don't have the answer, don't feel alone, neither did I.

One day I was preparing a meal for my children, my brother and Chris as I always did. I took pride in having a hot home cooked meal for my family each day. It was the one thing I felt made a house a home with everyone sharing a meal at the end of a long day. This particular day my brother and I stumbled into a conversation about good health and the importance of exercise. We both agreed we should do more to better our health. The conversation took a turn with an interesting twist form Chris. He made gestures and remarks about my cooking referring to the fact that I do it often but his comment was not in a good way but quite the contraire. He was making jokes about it in a way that along with all my cooking, I also eat too much. Then he went on and plugged in my weight. He chuckled at his own comments. I just joined in slightly laughing but with hurt feelings I concealed. Up to now, I didn't feel self-conscious about my size but quite confident. I felt funny now and it really left me wondering if maybe I should do something to lose a few pounds. After all, I wanted to keep my man. So I joined a gym dedicated to shedding some pounds. I had a vigorous routine of going to work, working out, and taking care of Chris and my children. I was determined to be the woman he wanted me to be. I really didn't realize what this relationship was doing to my self-esteem, but I continued because I wanted this. I took good care of Chris. I was very attentive to his needs. I made sure he had clean clothes, home cooked meals, laid his clothes out for him daily. This wasn't a stretch for me because I was just being me. I was patient with the time when I would see appreciation from Chris. Surely if I continued to give him my best, he would see how much love went into everything I did.

The relationship started to become a struggle. Working together was not as fun anymore. As I reflect back, we were in a relationship but we stop dating each other. Date nights came to a halt. Although I really couldn't put my finger on anything in particular, I still knew our relationship was on the rocks. So I decided to take matters in my own hands. I was a woman determined to preserve what we had. So I kicked it up a notch. I was more understanding to Chris thinking maybe he was just going through a little something and needed some male time. There were times I felt maybe I needed to turn it up in the bedroom. I left no stone unturned. I was fighting for us to work.

One evening after putting the children to bed, I decided it was time for a romantic evening. Lingerie, candles, and rose petals set the mood for this escape. I dressed to heighten the passion for my man topping it off with six inch heels. We needed this night.

I knew it would rekindle our love for each other. Chris came home and I was ready to ravish him kissing him from his lips down to his hard… Unbuttoning his shirt, I could feel his heart pumping through his chest. He wanted me and this boosted my ego to whip out some whip cream and play with his body with my tongue. I was in control and I knew I had him like putty in my hands. "This is my man," I thought to myself as I repeatedly satisfied him. We made love until we were panting for air. We both collapsed on either side of the bed lying next to each other exhaling.

When we arose the next morning by the sunlight in our faces, I rolled over to lie in my man's arms only for him to ask that I move over because he was hot and needed some air. I was a little stunned by this especially after the night we just had. I quickly pushed the thought to the side. I didn't want anything to ruin the moment, even though Chris already did. Later we went out to eat. I was so happy to be with him, I forgot the about the awkward morning we had. I broke my diet during this outing because I was really enjoying myself. It had been awhile since we had been out so I cherished this time we spent.

The next day I hit the gym with full force. I was so proud of myself. I sweated calories galore. I ran home to see Chris because I wanted him to see how hard I had been working on my body. I ran in the house to get water and before I could get a drink, I heard Chris yell out my name. I rush to see what he wanted. He asked me what was on the buffet. I'm thinking to myself, "Does he really think I been out eating all this time?" There I stand in confusion. He made reference again to me being out eating at the buffet. I was so hurt. I turned and walked away. He laughed and said he was only joking. There were those hurtful remarks again that he thought was okay in the form of joking. I didn't know why he was doing this, but I did know love wasn't supposed to be that way.

Later that evening, he announces that he and his best friend Stacy were going to the club that night. I also decided to go out too with my sister. So we agreed to all meet there. We danced all night. We were having a great time. I gave Chris a lap dance and I felt so sexy at the response I was getting from him.

The next day we were leaving work and it was Friday. Time to step out again and really give it the last day of the work week showdown as we always did. I asked Chris with excitement about the plans for the evening still hyped by the night before. I felt our relationship was slowly getting back to the good times. He looked at me with this unusual grin and said he wasn't taking me anywhere because I didn't know how to act. He referred to the night before when I gave him the lap dance. My heart dropped in amazement that this man could turn and change faces at a blink. I was giving up because nothing I seemed to do pleased this man. But you know what, I continued to work out and take care of myself. I lost weight and my clothes started to fit loose. I was doing so well. I look for compliments from him but instead he turned again. This time instead of fat, he tells me I look like a crack head. And again he laughs as all the times before. But oh yeah, he's only joking. This was starting to affect me and I didn't know how much more of this I wanted to deal with. The problem was I was in love with this man and emotionally attached to this abusive situation. Up, down, bad, good, I was so confused from one day to the next. I had the crazy notion that if I stayed things may change. I didn't want to give up. I wanted to hang in there and make it work.

Who was I fooling?

It was Chris that came to the conclusion that we should take a break and live separate for a while. Hesitantly I agreed, and I think I did out of sheer exhaustion. He promised that we would still see each other and work on things. It did get better. I even started receiving the sweet morning texts again.

We would lie in bed, after the close of another fun filled family night holding each other like we once did. Things seem to be good again. No doubt they had both been rocky but the hardest part about trusting him again was the proof of the past. Chris asked me why did I leave. As baffled and confused I was with him asking the obvious, I responded explaining to him how unloved I had begun to feel. I passionately expressed to him the pain and anger I felt with all of the verbal abuse I endured. Most of all, I had grown weary of the uncertainty of our future. I had to look out not only for my future but also my children's future.

I made the best decision I felt at the time was the only decision to move on with my life. After such a heartfelt summary of the pieces of my torn life, he asked me where I got the money to move. Not at all the response I was expecting but knowing Chris, this wasn't very farfetched. So I indulged. I told him I returned the engagement ring he gave me several months ago. We had plans to be married but our relationship was always so unpredictable. I didn't see any point to holding on. He let out somewhat of a frustrated sigh but managed to hold back what he was really feeling. He took a deep breath and said that it was alright. Now that probably wasn't what he wanted to say but that's what came out.

Pushing these thoughts back I began to devise a master plan to bring us all back together. Love controlled me when it came to this man. I was on a seesaw and I didn't know how to get off. Once again I packed up our lives, my children, and me giving this life with Chris yet another chance. I sold all my furniture to get as much money as I could for the move. Again I didn't tell anyone because I knew what they would say…"Why are you giving up your three bedroom place to live in his cramped space?" I went on anyway. Going on with my plans, we were able to move into the apartment the following month. When that time came, we did everything as scheduled. I sold most of my items because I had to down size from a three bedroom to fit into the one bedroom apartment Chris had. My boys had to sleep in the living room on a sofa. They really didn't question things. They just followed mom whenever, wherever. Surely this time would be the last one. I would think to myself as we settled in our new place. As much as I enjoyed these times, Chris was somewhat distance but not abusive. This was a new thing. He didn't really talk much. I can't say it was a bad thing, just a weird thing. He was still affectionate but seemed miles away. There were a few things I had to adjust to though. Chris had new rules. He was Muslim now. I must say I was stunned by this. I had no clue. He never mentioned this before. As I was unpacking, I was going to hang family portraits. Chris stopped me in my tracks. He didn't allow portraits because they may carry spirits. But wait! There's more. He didn't want pork or alcohol in the house. I tried to accept all these new ideas but many days I just needed a glass of wine. Our relationship was far from perfect and I missed my time of escape. Growing quite weary of this new thing, I decided I needed to make some changes of my own. I changed my work hours so I would have some time to myself away from Chris. I found a sitter for my children and I started working a dayshift. I was hanging out with my friends and I felt like my life had returned to normal. Some nights I would crash with a bag of food at the end of a night on the town. I guess it was stored up so long trying to live by such unrealistic rules. Well they were to me. I mean I'm not knocking that lifestyle but it wasn't for me.

 Chris would come home and be angered by the evidence of me being out with my friends but I didn't care anymore. I was getting fed up with him anyway by now. He changed moods more than underwear so I was very use to it. So my attitude was nonchalant.

The next morning, I was all dolled up and ready for work expecting a compliment from Chris. I had on my long ponytail feeling real cute. He blurted out a remark that I was going to get arrested. I clinched my chest asking why. He said for robbing horses. He was referring to my hair. I played it off like it didn't bother me. When I got into my car I cried. My feelings were hurt. I'm thinking to myself, "What can I do to please this man." When I was alone, I cried my eyes sore. When I was around others, I wore a smile. I wasn't the only one with a front. Chris was a perfect gentleman in front of others and a abuser behind closed doors. Abuse is not always a lick. Sometimes it's the words that fall out of a person's mouth onto another's heart.

He stopped buying groceries. He bought only what he wanted to eat. If he did buy for the children, he made sure it wasn't any for me. One day he purposely bought food I was allergic to. Tears began to roll down my face while I grabbed my keys, scraped up some money and went to get something to eat. All I wanted to know from God was, "Where do I go from here?"

The time had come to plan my son's birthday party. I was short on cash but I really wanted this to be special. Mothers always find a way to produce something out of nothing. I decided to have his party at the sitter's with all of the kids already there. My son wanted a bike but I couldn't afford to get it. I was so frustrated with all the details of pulling this together. Chris and I were barely speaking but I needed his help. I called him and he agreed to help and be at the party at the designated time. He arrived and had new outfits for the boys and I was about to pass out when he pulled out of his car a brand new bike. I hugged and kissed him. He saved the day. It had appeared that things were back to normal and I was happy.

Later, Chris expressed to me that he was tired of working at the casino and wanted to venture with starting his own business. He has researched it and talked it over with a relative. He was advised of how to break in and really make some good money. Along with this new ambition, Chris pulls out a ring. It really wasn't your traditional proposal. He just sort of told me we were going to get married. So I agreed not wanting to rock the boat since things were going well.

Chris left his job and I continued to work. Things were not at all like I expected. Instead of Chris putting time in getting his business going, he was sleeping and loafing around the house all day. I would come home to a dump. Clothes were all over the floor. He had not done anything all day. Several days of this had occurred. Furthermore, how were we going to plan a wedding and our future on the one income? I had begun to think this whole thing was a joke. Not to mention, I had not met any of Chris' family. He never invited me to any of the family functions. On rare occasions, I would talk to his mother. I decided to invite her for dinner so I could tell her the news. She had a strange response. She wanted to know if we told some character named Big Larry. I learned this was a good friend of Chris. But still not the response I had expected I'm looking like, what? I went on to find out she didn't know that Chris and I lived together. After the dinner, I went home and Chris was very inquisitive wanting to know all the details of what we talked about. I knew from that moment on, I really didn't know this man at all. Chris would not commit to setting a date to get married. I knew in my heart something was not right.

One day without notice he blurted out that he wanted a daughter. I was astonished. He felt he was getting older and wanted to complete our family with a baby girl. I had no idea these were his thoughts but I can truly say they were never my thoughts. All sorts of things were going through my head. I was concerned about my weight. Then I shifted to the ups and downs of our past.

My mind was racing. I felt like I was in a fool's paradise. I didn't really give him an answer then we went on with that totally unsettled. As time went on, here we go again, with the mood swings. I loved Chris but didn't know how to handle what he wanted. I began to blame myself for not trusting him enough to just go ahead and try for a baby girl. After all he accepted my sons and now he wanted a child of his own with me. I'm thinking maybe it will be okay. And just maybe this will be the happy ending we needed. I pondered many days as I watched Chris grow more and more distant. So I decided to stop taking my birth control pills despite all my reservations. Chris started a new job and a few months later I was hired too. Still not being able to connect with this man, I moved out again because Chris was in a world of his own. I was so confused. Even though I wasn't on the pill anymore as he requested, it was still a crazy time for us.

Giving him what he wanted wasn't enough to hold him in a happy place. I was blessed once again with a very nice townhouse. Chris and I continued our relationship and rode to work together.

A great deal of time had passed. The thought of having a baby wasn't discussed anymore although I felt it was locked away in a small part of his mind.

What can I say?

I was wrong. I say this because I did in fact conceive. I told Chris the news and he seemed to fake his excitement. This was confusing because he had requested this desire. Even though we hadn't said much about it recently, I felt confident he would be happy with the news .The next phase was like walking in the dark feeling my way through to know what move to make next.

One day we decided to plan a getaway for a few days .We went to the casino, played and enjoyed ourselves .When we returned home, I witnessed, something that that I knew wasn't normal but even today I can't believe the mood swings of this man. He was in the bathroom which seemed an eternity. I'm waiting patiently because I wanted to go and grab a bite to eat. Finally, anxiously, with a slightly elevated voice I told him I was hungry. His response was "You set me up .You got pregnant on purpose." I'm thinking well yes, as you requested. I couldn't believe this. I asked God to please help me.

Three days later, I began to spot blood. I was home alone. Christ was at work. I drove myself to the hospital. I was examined and given the news that my baby had no heartbeat. I was placed in a room where I filled two large pads with blood waiting for medical personnel to tell me what to do next.

I tried calling Chris again and again. Still he never showed up. I was losing my baby and all he could offer me was that he was out on the town with some coworkers. The nurse prepared me to check out with a lifeless baby in my belly. She gave me a number for an outpatient surgery. You see, back then you could be refused care if you lacked insurance. I had Tennessee Insurance but I was in Mississippi Hospital. I went on to the hospital that would do the procedure. I was hurt as any mother would be. In my thoughts, I knew it was probably for the best which was my comfort.

Chapter seven

False Faces

It was class reunion time again. I needed to get away by myself and away from Chris. I plan this trip only with April in mind...

Even though Chris and I lived separately, we still spent most of our days and nights together, which led to me moving back in with him. I was on a merry go round giving up my home and all my nice stuff to give this another chance. Our lives were very much intertwined.

I had asked Chris before I made plans if he wanted to go with me to my class reunion. He said no. At first I was disappointed but quickly was over it with the thought of a real vacation from it all. One of my friends was going and it worked out for us to ride together. When the day of departure arrived I grabbed my bags and proceeded to leave without any questions or gestures of a good bye or anything from Chris. I thought maybe he would miss me but his reaction was that he could care less. Only thing I gained from trying to reach out to him at the moment was that he still had the power to make me feel bad. I walked out the door promising myself that I would still have a good time as planned. I had a marvelous time. I danced until I dropped. I enjoyed seeing everyone again. Word was we were the best class ever, Class of 94. The last day of the event we all met up at a restaurant and said our farewells. I hated to see it end. Back home I went. My friend and I laughed all the way home of the time we had. Right in the middle of the laughter, I realized what I was going home to. My friend immediately noticed my sadness. She knew I didn't want to go and she felt sad for me too.

I got out of the car with tears in my eyes grabbed my bags and dragged inside. I dropped my bags there at the door thinking Chris would at least help me in. He looked at me and continued to do what he was doing. As I began to unpack he then decided to ask if I had fun. So I eagerly responded that it was an amazing time. So then he asks why I didn't invite him. I wasn't in the mood for that foolishness. I immediately ended that conversation because it didn't take a psychic to know where that was leading. I left back out to go pick up my children whom I missed so much. They were happy to see me too. We got snacks and headed home. After spending a little time with them it grew late so I put them to bed. Chris wanted to talk. I talked a little sharing the events of my trip with him. He reached out to me as if he wanted to sleep in his arms. So I obliged and soon we fell asleep.

I jumped up early the next morning excited to get my pictures developed. As I was showing them to Chris he had this weird look on his face. So I asked him why he was looking like that. He pointed at my ring finger on the pictures. I had removed it from my left hand to my right hand.

I didn't want anyone asking me about it, especially since I felt the whole engagement was a phase. Chris was very angry at this. But the crazy thing about this was I couldn't imagine what else he expected. We weren't exactly love birds these days, quite the opposite. How could he possibly think that I would want to show off that ring with the way he had been treating me. I told him that when he proposed, I had great hopes of us being a family and living a happy life. But numerous of occasions he stumped on my dreams. This man acted as if all of this was news to him and he wasn't a participant in this hell we lived in. He went days like this. He displayed depression and walked around the house like I had pierced his soul. I didn't know what to make of this. As crazy as this sounds, and as much as this man hurt me, I felt guilty and responsible for his apparent pain. So actively forgetting the suffering he put me through the first time I was pregnant, I began to remember his wish for a daughter. I can't tell you how I justified this in my mind but I did. Truth of the matter is, I still loved this man. I had the ability to separate the bad from the good having the good make a stand. The bad that happen when he denied me and our dead baby with no benefit of his support and comfort went out the window right with my good judgment. Despite all he put me through, I hated to see him this hurt knowing I caused it. So I planned to make it up to him. I wanted to get pregnant in hopes of having a girl. Yes I know what you must think. But at the time, my mind was just as broken as my heart. Also I still loved him. It was October and I began to get the closeness back. I tried to cheer up Chris. I did everything I could to pull him out of the slump he was in. I would work the rest of the time dealing with the sadness in that house. I was so stressed. My hair was shedding and I fell into depression of my own. Believe or not I moved out again.

During the height of this drama, I did some stepping out of my own. I spent time with a man I worked with. He took me down a road that made me realize I may as well deal with what I had with Chris. At least that was my reasoning at the time. I went through many changes coming out of this affair, including ending an unwanted pregnancy.

Even so Chris still was a part of our lives. I don't know why I couldn't move on from this man. A couple of months passed and I just threw my hands up because I needed to admit to myself, I wasn't going to live my life without Chris. All of this back and forth, moving in and out, starting over only to be right back living with him again.

It was total madness. From this point on it, was no more denying it. I loved him and still wanted him. But most of all I wanted to have his baby. I shared this with a friend. She thought I was really losing it but I was serious as one could be. I made peace with my feelings. All that Chris and I had been through, nothing kept me away. I always accepted him back. I know that sounds crazy. But at the time it was more crazy to continue to fooling myself that I would actually leave Chris for good. So this is where I end this cycle of confusion, grab my man and fix this mess. Years had passed. It was time to take charge over our future. It was December approaching Christmas and what better gift for Chris than the news that we are going to start that family he wanted. We were all going to be a family and I was determined that this would work.

After launching my plan, I felt it was time to see if I have the perfect gift, right on time as scheduled. My pregnancy test was positive. My plan was working out perfectly. I told Chris the news and waited for his response. I knew it would be good because I planned the way I would announce it to ensure nothing but a joyful return.

My plan fell through Chris was upset. A apparently he had changed his mind about having a child. Yes I did take a chance. His attitude with the last pregnancy should have been the breaking point to perish this notion of a daughter bringing him happiness, but it didn't. I was blind. My dream was shattered and I was back down to earth to face the haunting reality that this was the real Chris dogging me the same as the time when I lost our first baby. I didn't know what to do. Now that I was out of the clouds, I was dealing with another reality, I was pregnant.

If that wasn't enough, Chris suggested an abortion. So since I was very much responsible for this all, I agreed to have the abortion. Four days later, Chris called with a change of heart. He felt we should do the right thing and have the baby. I shared with him the sickness that I usually have being pregnant and my concerns for going to work.

Morning came and I got the children off to school. He told me to put my notice in at work and from now on my job is to have a healthy baby and care for the boys. He was sitting me down. He wanted me and the boys to move back in with him. Chris and I talked some more. He was going to transfer to a bigger apartment. He expressed he didn't want the children sleeping on the sofa anymore and I agreed I answered yes and wasn't thinking at the time I had signed a new lease. I had just finished furnishing my place and really started to pick up the pieces of my broken life. In spite of that I loved everything I was hearing. I guess my plan worked out after all. With those words, I left everything to join him. I can't tell you how excited I felt. This was truly it. We were going to be happy.

Chapter eight

The Pull

It was time to decorate and put my ladies touch to this situation. Chris was attentive to my needs. He was very careful to keep my stress down. He wanted me to have a good pregnancy. I was at home and all I had to be concerned about was staying healthy. I took my leave from work and began to be a stay home mom. Chris decided to work another part time job with his mother at the store for extra money for the family. Everything was falling into place...

I received a call. It was his sister expressing she hadn't seen Chris in some days. I didn't say much. I hung up and called Chris. I really didn't get much from him. He didn't mention not going to the store. I hung up wondering where he was going if not to work.

I didn't ask him anything because I didn't want to stir up anything since everything was so perfect. So I just observed things to see what else I could find out. I was going through the usual symptoms of pregnancy trying to remain calm. Things slowly showed signs of the old days.

My routine was pretty monotonous. I ate. I slept. Mostly I felt neglected. I didn't feel any affection from Chris. He didn't talk much and the silence was disturbing. I knew the routine of another mood swinging episode. I began to cringe, begging God to please not let this happen again, not now. Chris hanged out with friends leaving my children and me alone many nights. I just did what I needed to do to get by.

One Sunday coming home from church, I was hit by a man that damaged my car leaving it unsafe to drive. It was in bad shape too, but I had no choice. It was all I had to transport my children so I accepted it. The air was broken and this was during one of the hottest summers. I can remember I was pregnant riding in this scorching hot truck. Sweat dripping, legs stuck to the leather seats it was miserable. My children and I believed there were better days ahead.

Day after Day was the same. Night after night I would end the day crying myself to sleep.

One night at about one in the morning, I was awakened by a phone call from Chris. He informed me he needed to discuss something with me. I fell asleep again with thoughts of wondering what was so urgent.

Chris came home and I was awakened with a shake. He was ready to talk. I wobbled up to sit in the bed listening to him. He announced that he would not be living with us anymore. My eyes were fixated on him in complete amazement. He said he would go on paying the bills as he always has done. He just requested that I pay my own cell bill. I was numb. I didn't move or respond. I felt as if the wind was knocked from my lungs and I would never breathe again. I fell back down with showers of my tears saturating my face rolling onto my pillow. My mother called that morning, but I couldn't even tell her what happened. I managed to get "hello" out. She sensed something was wrong. She feared that I was about to throw in the towel. She said God told her to tell me to go ahead and take the pull, because he will pull you out. I cried as I hung up the phone. Chris left early that day and that was his last day there. In my heart, I felt abandoned and thrown away. How many times have I given up my life to give this man another chance? And now at my most vulnerable time, he leaves me. That is what I felt then. But now I do know that was God ending that cycle for me. I would have never had the strength to do it. He answered my prayers but it wasn't the answer I thought he would deliver. Now I was left to figure out how we would make it, my children, me, and baby on the way. I wasn't working and it was all I could do to make ends meet with the government assistance I had coming in. My son discovered he had a cousin that lived across the street. I gathered my children and we walked over there hoping to get some help. We were welcomed in and we were told we could come over anytime. I learned to survive from my son's cousin. I learned to stretch my coins to get the things we needed. We didn't have much but we kept going. My sister came to visit often. She and her children spent nights with us. My sister would lie on the floor at night beside my bed. She didn't have a car so it worked out because her job was close to my house. I would give her a ride to work. We helped each other. As my pregnancy grew near, I was unable to drive, so I loaned her my car so she could continue to get to work. I still had the truck, so it didn't matter as much.

I continued going to church so I wouldn't give up on myself. My children needed me. I would receive calls from Chris telling me I had thirty days to move out of the house. He was reneging on his promise. I had no job, no money, and no reliable car. I just was just getting by with what we had. We had nowhere to go. I thought often of suicide. I had thoughts of just jumping from my bedroom window which was upstairs.

I perceived thoughts of just ending it to get out of this misery. I would get a razor and swipe cut my stomach until it bled. I was down to my last when my sister came up with a proposition to buy that old car I had. We made an agreement and that was same take financial help for me.

As I got further into my pregnancy, Chris took me back and forth to my doctor's appointments but showed no interest in my well being or the baby. He and his family created the idea that the baby was not his. Although his mom was kind to me when I called, she still never showed any concern for us. Chris slowly stopped paying the bills and I began to receive notices in the mail reflecting no payment.

I would call Chris and each time I would get the same answer. It wasn't long, he completely stopped and I was left with no support. His mom helped once but after that I was on my own.

One amazing Sunday there was an alter call for individuals that needed help with utility bills. I slowly rose out of my seat moving forward to the front to stand with a few others. After the minister prayed over us, he blessed us with funds to cover the bills of everyone at the altar. All I could do is breakdown and cry tears of gratitude. This was truly a blessing.

Moving forward with my pregnancy I wanted to plan a baby shower in hopes of getting some things I needed for the new baby. My mom and a friend helped me to get things together I was so excited anticipating this big day. My mom and I were enjoying one another and suddenly there was a knock at the door. It was someone Chris and his aunt sent over to do some work on the house. She was the owner. Soon after, his aunt pulls up. My mom and I left them in the house and we went on with our day together. It was such a hot day but we had so much fun. When we returned home I just fell out to cool off. I woke up in horrible sweat.

It was later; I discovered the air wasn't working. I was frantic because this was the day before my baby shower. I called a repair man but he didn't seem to know what was wrong. We decided to move the shower to my sister's house. I was very disappointed but I had no choice. As we prepared to move, my neighbor called out to me. She told me some very disturbing news. The aunt had maintenance workers to unplug wires to sabotage the air to force us out. She didn't want me or my family living there anymore. Even though she tried her best to ruin my day, I still had a nice baby shower at my sister apartment.

At this time my house was so hot. I had to move out. I moved in with one of my sisters. My children and I slept on sofa sleeper. It was crowded and uncomfortable but I enjoyed being around family. Much to my surprise, Chris offered to get us an apartment.

My sister convinced her landlord to give me a chance. Chris put his name on the apartment and I got approved to move in my apartment. By now I was eight month along, so I had to hurry and get my place ready. My family helped me. I worked diligently getting things in order. Once he signed the lease, I didn't hear much from him.

We enjoyed our new place. We went through a lot to get there. We settled in very well with the closeness of my family around me again. As the days passed, I went to my last doctor's visit. I was given my date to have a cesarean. I felt a little lonely surrounded by couples but I made it through. I was relieved to get a date for this to be over. I called Chris to inform him and he nonchalantly said ok.

I went home to prepare my family and my children for the date of my baby's arrival. When the day arrived I was so nervous that Chris wouldn't show up to take me to the hospital, but he did.

He didn't come to the door to get me, he blew the horn. So I grabbed my bag and headed to the car. When we got to the hospital he walked ahead of me, leaving me behind to walk alone. The nurse proceeded to check me in noticing Chris was leaving. She was puzzled asking me if he was really leaving. I just nodded. She went on to prep me for the delivery of my baby girl.

The pain was coming on strong, but the emotional pain was even stronger. I cried, not only from the pain of birthing, but also from feeling lonely and worthless.

Thank God the nurses comforted me. Before I knew it, I heard my baby cry. The doctor placed her in my arms and all I could feel was joy and relief. After a few moments of bonding, the nurse took my baby so I could rest. After resting I call my mom to tell her the news. She knew all the pain I had endured during the pregnancy. My mom was crying and yelling "Thank God you and the baby made it through. From this day forward, the choice is yours to continue to take the pull." I had to do something different.

After I had my baby, God blessed me with employment, a new car, and a new mindset. Chris moved on doing what he always did which didn't amount to nothing. I was delivered from his strong hold moving on with my life. He eventually married and later divorced. We were working at the same casino again. I watched him every day trying to flaunt his women in my face. It didn't bother me like he planned because he was completely out of my system. Being on the outside looking in, I realized he didn't want anything out of life. He was satisfied with the way he lived his life. However, I wanted more.

The Awakening

Sitting in my living room after a long day, I decided to not go out. I felt I deserved to spend time with me. As much as I enjoy the glimmer of the night life, it dropped in my spirit to stay put. I made myself a drink, put my feet up and began to unwind. Before my thoughts could drift to dreams, my guardian angel tapped me on my shoulder to ask me a life changing question. "How long are you going to allow these men to dictate your destiny?" My body began to shake as tears ran down my face. I knew it was the presence of the Lord. The Holy Spirit began to minister to me. I wasn't afraid because I always felt his presence but now I heard his voice. I couldn't answer the question as I cried louder. As I pondered in my mind an answer, I heard the voice of God through angels speak on my behalf....

Oh April, How long must you do this? How long must you put your trust in men and not your Creator? Angels from on high were having a conversation about me...

They discussed me and I could hear them in my spirit. One said "Let's give her a little more time to figure this thing out." Another said, "But she hasn't yet, and I can't watch her continue knowing we have so much more for her." Another said, "God has chosen her and he gave us an assignment which is to protect her."

The first angel finally agreed. At this time God dispatched the angles to come and comfort me. I know now I must be about my journey to find out my purpose. Because if God loved me so much, he brought me through all of this, there must be a higher calling for me. My story doesn't end here. It begins here. I realize I need to change paths. With God's help, I will.

To all of my sisters…. It's not where you come from. It's not even about what you are doing now. But it's about where you are going. It's about arrival and fulfilling your purpose. The angels left this message with me…"Wait on God for your perfect mate. Meanwhile, fall in love with April. Allow God to be the man in your life. Allow the showers of your tears to water and nurture your future. For every tear you have cried fell into God's Hands."

A Work in Progress

Sitting around talking about the past and future, my friends and I realized we are truly blessed. We make a point to slow down the pace from time to time to spend some quality time together and just talk, have some coffee, and good food. It feels good to connect with other strong women not afraid to tell their testimonies. Why be ashamed of a victory? If you went through the fire and came out not burned, then someone needs to know that. I remember when I didn't even want to live anymore. I had been through so much. I believed there was no more for me in this life. God blessed me with my own set of angels to keep me safe from myself.

I have a ways to go as I continue my journey of finding my purpose. On the path of finding out what's true, I have encountered on many occasions the counterfeit version. I'm still striving toward the mark. Raising my children, I depend on God. Now I didn't say I was perfect but I am real.

Working everyday with my goals in mind, I am reminded of the day when I didn't have basic necessities to live. I can truly say to the next single parent…Hold on and take the pull. If you make that first step, God will carry you the rest of the way. I am a living testimony of what He can and will do for you.

Religion is something one may practice as a way of life but I have found that it is what is in your heart that reaches the Creator.

Telling my story, I revealed many avenues of wrong choices and decisions I made. I don't regret anything. All that I have endured gave me the strength and wisdom to pass on to the next person.

Back to the girl talk I shared with my friends. As spiritual women, we know that we have purpose to have survived horrifying events. We reflect back knowing we should have been dead or crazy but instead we are strong women of valiant. We have seen angels, been spoken to by God and experienced life changing events.

As I close, I want to leave this with you. Until you have tapped into what you are created for, in other words, your purpose, there will be days of doubting your destiny. Once you have learned what that special purpose is, you can begin a journey of fulfilment.

As a work in progress, I believe God's promise for me will come to pass and I will reign in my purpose.

Made in the USA
Monee, IL
29 October 2021